Warships

Rob Colson

Published in paperback in 2014 by Wayland
Copyright © Wayland 2014

Wayland
338 Euston Road
London NW1 3BH

Wayland Australia
Level 17/207 Kent Street
Sydney NSW 2000

All rights reserved.
Senior editor: Julia Adams
Produced by Tall Tree Ltd
Editor, Tall Tree: Jon Richards
Designer: Ed Simkins

British Library Cataloguing in Publication Data

Colson, Robert.
  Warships. -- (Ultimate machines)
  1. Warships--Juvenile literature.
  I. Series
  623.8'225-dc23

ISBN: 978 0 7502 8140 9

Printed in China

10 9 8 7 6 5 4 3 2 1

Wayland is a division of Hachette Children's
Books, an Hachette UK company.
www.hachette.co.uk

Picture credits
Cover main US Navy, cover bl Antony Platt/
Dreamstime.com , cover br US Navy, 1 US
Navy, 2 US Navy, 4 Myriam Thyes, 5t Viva-Verdi/
Creative Commons, 5b US Navy, 6 Jitloac/
Dreamstime.com, 7t Photos.com, 7b Rcbutcher,
8-9 US Navy, 8t US Navy, 9t US Navy, 10t US
Navy, 10b US Navy, 11 US Navy, 12-13 US Navy,
13t US Navy, 13b US Navy, 14-15 US Navy,
15t US Navy, 15b US Navy, 16-17 Geo Swan/
GNU, 16t Caela Søndrol/GNU, 17t Kristoffer
Ruud Røgeberg, 18 US Navy, 19t US Navy, 19b
US Navy, 20 Trinity Mirror/Mirrorpix/Alamy, 21t
US Navy, 21b BAE Systems, 24 Geo Swan/GNU

Contents

War at sea

Warships are machines designed to fight at sea. They carry guns and are protected by armour. Warships are built to be fast and easy to manoeuvre.

Modern navies use many different types of warship. Some warships, such as destroyers, patrol the seas and attack enemy ships. Others, such as aircraft carriers, are designed to carry planes, while submarines are warships that move underwater.

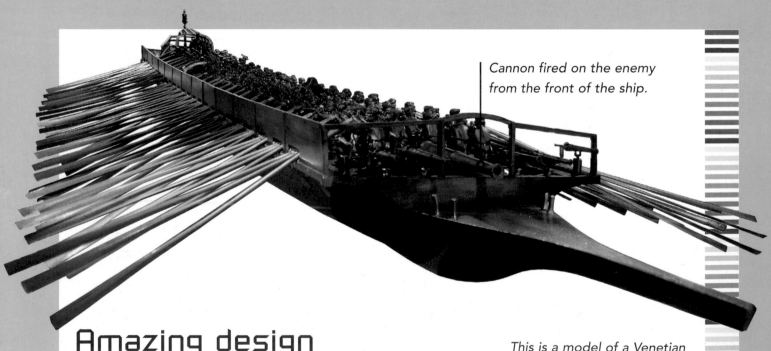

Cannon fired on the enemy from the front of the ship.

Amazing design

Galleys were an early type of warship. They were powered by lines of rowers pulling on oars. Galleys were first developed more than 2,000 years ago, and were used in sea battles right up to the 1500s. The front, or bow, of the ship was fitted with a battering ram. The ships would move towards the enemy side-by-side so that they could protect each other's unarmed sides, or flanks.

This is a model of a Venetian galley from the 1200s. It was powered by more than 100 oarsmen.

Age of sail

As well as being powered by oars, early warships used large sails to catch the wind. HMS *Victory* was a large sail-powered warship. It was launched in 1765, and had a crew of more than 800 men. Sail-powered warships dominated the seas until the mid-1800s, when they were replaced by steam-powered ships.

HMS Victory carried 104 guns, most of which were lined up in rows along the ship's sides.

The USS Kidd is a type of warship known as a guided-missile destroyer. Modern warships such as this are powered by turbine engines, which turn a propeller at the back of the ship.

Ironclad

An ironclad was a steam-powered ship whose body, or hull, was covered and protected by thick plates of iron or steel.

HMS *Warrior* was built in 1860 and was one of the first ironclad ships. This new type of ship was faster and more powerful than the sail-powered warships that had been used before.

As well as a steam engine, HMS Warrior had three masts to hold sails.

Old wooden ships such as the one on the left were not as well protected as HMS Warrior (shown on the right).

Extra protection

The outside of HMS *Warrior*'s hull was covered in thick iron sheets. Inside the ship was another layer of protection. A huge metal box held the ship's steam engine and all of its powerful guns. This box was made from sheets of iron that were 12 cm thick. The boat was also divided up into watertight compartments. These stopped water spreading if a hole was made in the outer hull.

Amazing design

HMS *Warrior* was powered by a coal-fired engine. A coal fire heated water to make steam. The steam powered the engine, which turned a propeller at the back of the ship. HMS *Warrior* also had masts and sails to provide extra power and to move the ship if its engine broke. Steam-powered ships were faster than those that only had sails.

The ship's engine had huge pistons such as the one shown here. The pistons were pushed in and out by the force of the steam.

Iowa class battleship

Battleships were large warships that carried powerful guns. These guns could fire shells over great distances.

Iowa class battleships were built for the US Navy during World War II. The ships were named after the first to be built, the USS *Iowa*. These fast battleships were in service until 1991.

Firing broadside

The USS *Iowa* was fitted with nine guns mounted in turrets. The turrets could be swung round so that they all fired in the same direction. This is called firing broadside. The guns were 20 metres long, and fired shells over a range of 40 kilometres.

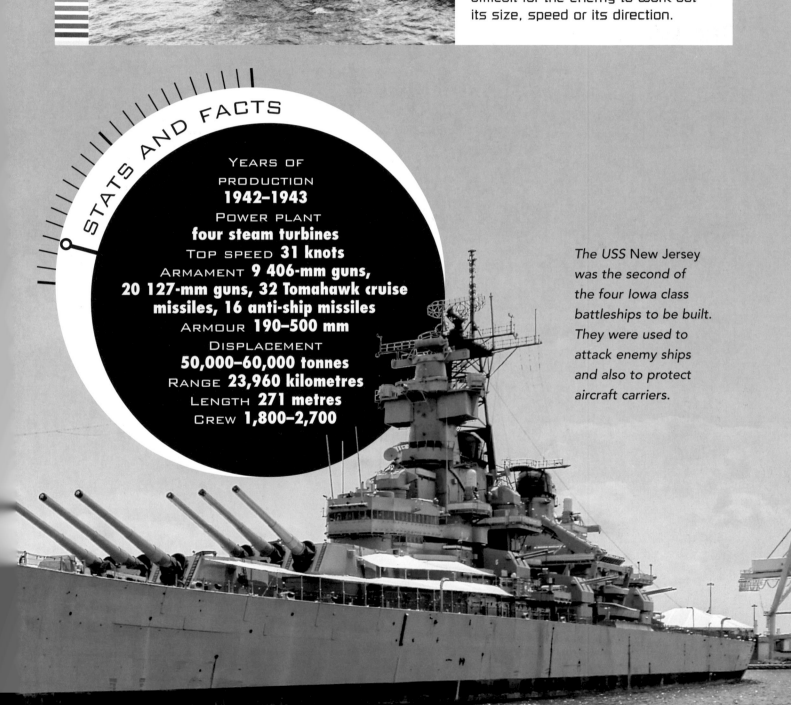

Amazing design

During World War II, the USS *Iowa* was painted with blue, black and grey camouflage to make it harder for enemy submarines to target it. Rather than hide the ship, the thick stripes were designed to make it difficult for the enemy to work out its size, speed or its direction.

STATS AND FACTS

YEARS OF PRODUCTION
1942–1943
POWER PLANT
four steam turbines
TOP SPEED **31 knots**
ARMAMENT **9 406-mm guns,
20 127-mm guns, 32 Tomahawk cruise
missiles, 16 anti-ship missiles**
ARMOUR **190–500 mm**
DISPLACEMENT
50,000–60,000 tonnes
RANGE **23,960 kilometres**
LENGTH **271 metres**
CREW **1,800–2,700**

The USS New Jersey *was the second of the four Iowa class battleships to be built. They were used to attack enemy ships and also to protect aircraft carriers.*

Cruisers

Cruisers are smaller and faster than battleships. Battleships are vulnerable to attack from modern missiles, so are no longer used. Cruisers are now the largest warships on the seas.

Cruisers perform a wide range of roles. They can attack other ships or defend a group, or convoy, of ships from enemy aircraft.

Kirov class

The Russian navy's Kirov class battlecruisers, such as the *Frunze* (left), are 252 metres long and have a crew of 710. These ships are powered by nuclear reactors and carry missiles that are designed to attack enemy ships.

Amazing design

Guided-missile cruisers in the US Navy are fitted with vertical launching systems (VLS). The missiles are stored in upright tubes. The missiles fire straight up into the air, then turn towards their targets once they are at a safe height. This system allows the ships to carry a large number of weapons in a small space.

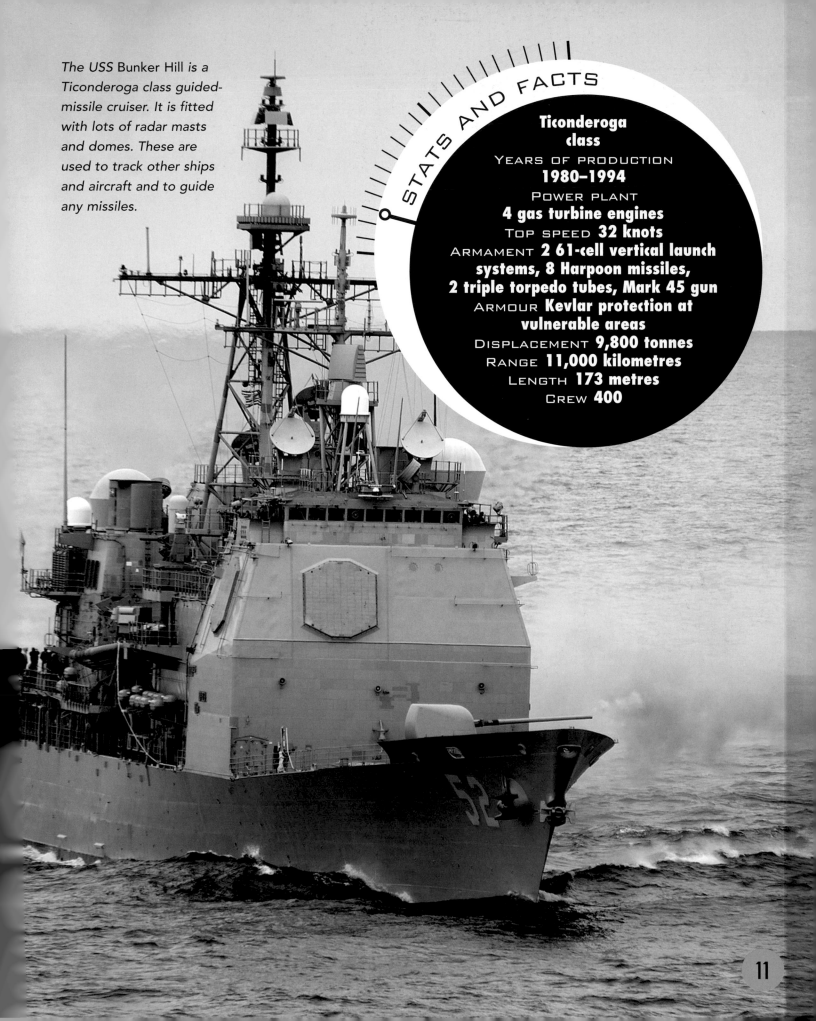

The USS Bunker Hill is a Ticonderoga class guided-missile cruiser. It is fitted with lots of radar masts and domes. These are used to track other ships and aircraft and to guide any missiles.

STATS AND FACTS

Ticonderoga class

YEARS OF PRODUCTION
1980–1994
POWER PLANT
4 gas turbine engines
TOP SPEED **32 knots**
ARMAMENT **2 61-cell vertical launch systems, 8 Harpoon missiles, 2 triple torpedo tubes, Mark 45 gun**
ARMOUR **Kevlar protection at vulnerable areas**
DISPLACEMENT **9,800 tonnes**
RANGE **11,000 kilometres**
LENGTH **173 metres**
CREW **400**

Aircraft carriers

Warships that carry planes and helicopters are called aircraft carriers. Nimitz class aircraft carriers in the US Navy are the largest military ships in the world.

Each ship has 3,200 sailors and 2,500 pilots and aircrew. They carry between 85 and 90 planes and helicopters.

The USS Abraham Lincoln *is one of ten Nimitz class carriers built for the US Navy.*

STATS AND FACTS

YEARS OF PRODUCTION **1975–2009**

POWER PLANT **Four nuclear reactors**

TOP SPEED **30 knots**

ARMAMENT **16–24 Sea Sparrow missiles, 3–4 Phalanx close-in weapons systems (CIWSs)**

ARMOUR **65 mm Kevlar**

DISPLACEMENT **106,300 tonnes**

RANGE **needs to refuel after 20 years**

LENGTH **333 metres**

CREW **5,700**

Air base at sea

Each Nimitz carrier transports a range of aircraft to perform various roles. These roles include attacking enemy aircraft and ground targets, detecting enemy ships, submarines and aircraft, and rescuing crashed pilots. There are two parts to the flight deck. The landing strip is angled at 9 degrees and the take-off strip is at the front of the ship. This means that planes can take off and land at the same time.

The aircraft are stored, serviced and repaired in a large hangar deck that is beneath the flight deck. They are carried up to the flight deck using large elevators.

Arrestor wires stop an F-18 Hornet after it lands on the carrier's deck.

Amazing design

While the carrier is 333 metres long, this is still not long enough for a fighter jet to take off and land normally. To take off, the aircraft need to use powerful catapults to gain enough speed so that they can lift off the flight deck. On landing, planes use a long hook behind them. This hook latches onto special cables, called arrestor wires, which slow the plane down.

Guided-missile frigates

A guided-missile frigate is a small warship designed to protect other ships from attack.

Oliver Hazard Perry class guided-missile frigates of the US Navy carry missiles to fire at aircraft and torpedoes to fire at submarines. These warships escort aircraft carriers or convoys of ships carrying valuable cargo.

The USS Carr is a 'long-hull' frigate. It is two metres longer than the standard Oliver Hazard Perry class, and carries larger helicopters.

STATS AND FACTS

YEARS OF PRODUCTION **1975–2004**

POWER PLANT **2 gas turbines**

TOP SPEED **29 knots**

ARMAMENT **anti-aircraft guided missiles, anti-ship missiles, 2 torpedo tubes, 1 rapid-fire cannon**

ARMOUR **19-mm Kevlar over vital areas**

DISPLACEMENT **4200 tonnes**

RANGE **8,300 kilometres at 20 knots**

LENGTH **136 metres**

CREW **176**

Targets

The frigates carry special missiles called drones that are guided using radio controls. The drones are used for target practice and they are powered by turbojet engines. When a drone's mission is completed, the engine is switched off and it parachutes into the sea to be recovered by another ship.

A BQM-74E drone is launched from USS Thach. Other ships pretend the drones are enemy missiles and practise shooting at them.

Amazing design

At the rear of each frigate is a helideck, where helicopters can land and take off. The helicopters are kept in hangars just in front of the helideck. They are used to rescue crashed pilots and to spot enemy submarines.

A Sea Hawk helicopter takes off from the USS Thach. An operator stands on the helideck and guides the pilot using hand signals.

Skjold class patrol boat

Patrol boats are small, fast warships designed to sail along the coast looking for enemy ships or smugglers.

Skjold class warships are the fastest armed craft in the world. These patrol boats were built for the Norwegian Navy and they are made of light but strong materials, such as carbon fibre.

Amazing design

The Skjold class is a stealth craft, which means that it has been designed to be hard to detect using radar. Radar works by sending out radio waves and then listening for the echo when the waves bounce off an object. Skjold class boats have angled sides that are designed to scatter radio waves so that they do not bounce back in the direction of the radar.

P961

Simulator

Skjold class warships are very fast and complex to control. This means that it would be dangerous to train sailors in the ships themselves. Instead, they are trained in a computer simulator. The simulator contains an exact replica of the ship's bridge, and computer-generated images in the windows show how the ship would be moving.

The Skjold class is a catamaran, which means that it has two parallel hulls. This means that less of the boat is in contact with the water, allowing it to travel faster than a boat with one large hull.

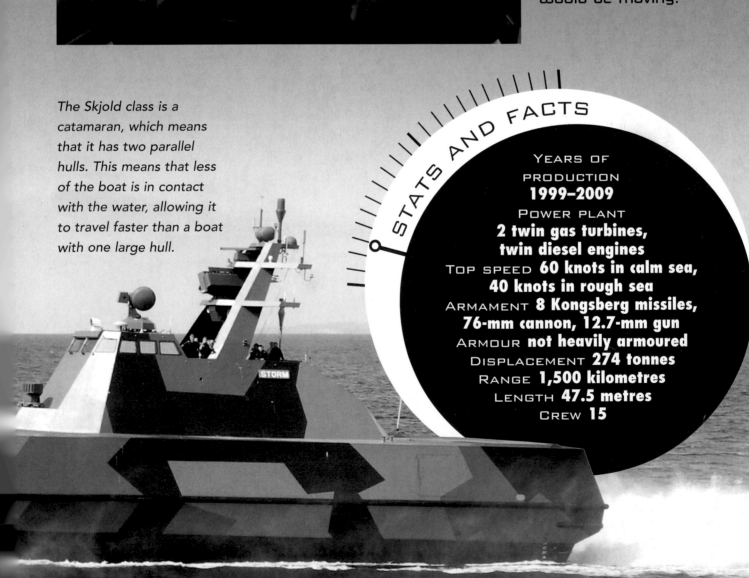

STATS AND FACTS

YEARS OF PRODUCTION
1999–2009
POWER PLANT
2 twin gas turbines, twin diesel engines
TOP SPEED **60 knots in calm sea, 40 knots in rough sea**
ARMAMENT **8 Kongsberg missiles, 76-mm cannon, 12.7-mm gun**
ARMOUR **not heavily armoured**
DISPLACEMENT **274 tonnes**
RANGE **1,500 kilometres**
LENGTH **47.5 metres**
CREW **15**

Amphibious assault ships

Amphibious assault ships look like small aircraft carriers. However, their main purpose is to transport troops that are going to make an attack on land.

Under the top deck, amphibious assault ships have a lower deck where they carry landing craft. The landing craft take troops and equipment to the shore.

Flight deck

The top deck of an amphibious assault ship is designed to carry aircraft. Large transporter helicopters carry troops and equipment to the battlefield. Aeroplanes able to take off vertically, such as Harrier jump jets, provide air support to the troops. The ships also carry smaller helicopters which protect the ships from submarine attacks.

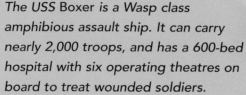

The USS Boxer is a Wasp class amphibious assault ship. It can carry nearly 2,000 troops, and has a 600-bed hospital with six operating theatres on board to treat wounded soldiers.

Amazing design

Landing craft are carried in the well deck, a lower deck at the rear, or stern, of the ship. During operations, the stern gate is opened and the ship lowers its stern by taking on water. This floods the well deck, allowing landing craft to dock inside the ship. The largest landing craft can carry up to 400 fully equipped soldiers. A ship may carry two large landing craft or several smaller ones.

STATS AND FACTS

Wasp class

YEARS OF PRODUCTION
1989–2006
POWER PLANT
2 gas turbines
TOP SPEED **22 knots**
ARMAMENT **4 missile launchers, 3 Phalanx CIWs**
ARMOUR **up to 100 mm**
DISPLACEMENT **41,150 tonnes**
RANGE **17,600 kilometres**
LENGTH **253 metres**
CREW **1,200 plus 1,900 troops**

The USS Essex leaves harbour to start a mission. Amphibious assault ships usually travel as part of a larger force that includes cruisers, destroyers and submarines.

Submarines

Warships called submarines travel underwater. This makes them very hard to detect.

Modern submarines can launch missiles at targets that are thousands of kilometres away, or they can hunt down and destroy enemy ships at close quarters.

An Astute class submarine can dive to depths of more than 250 metres. It can stay underwater for months at a time because it does not need to refuel.

STATS AND FACTS

Astute class

YEARS OF PRODUCTION
2007–present

POWER PLANT
nuclear reactor

TOP SPEED **more than 30 knots submerged**

ARMAMENT **6 torpedo tubes**

DISPLACEMENT **7,400 tonnes**

RANGE **limited only by the need to take on new food supplies for the crew**

LENGTH **97 metres**

CREW **98**

The USS K-2 was painted with camouflage to hide it when it had to come to the surface.

The first submarines spent most of their time on the surface, diving underwater only to attack ships. Many were sunk when they came to the surface by the ships they had been attacking.

Nuclear power

Early submarines were powered by diesel engines and had to surface regularly to refuel and to replace stale air. Modern submarines, such as the Royal Navy's Astute class submarines, are powered by nuclear reactors. They never have to be refuelled and they can stay underwater until they run out of supplies for the sailors on board.

Special acoustic tiles make the submarine invisible to sonar detectors.

Amazing design

Ships can see what is happening underwater using a sensor called sonar. This works by sending out sound waves. The waves bounce back off any objects in the water, and the ship listens out for the echo. The Astute class submarine is covered with special acoustic tiles. The tiles absorb the sound waves from the sonar, so none of the sound bounces back and the submarine remains hidden.

Glossary

amphibious
Able to move on land and on water. Amphibious assault ships launch attacks on land from the water.

boiler
A container of water that is heated to make steam.

bow
The front part of a ship.

camouflage
A pattern that is designed to make it difficult for enemies to spot an object.

cannon
A weapon that fires large metal balls.

carbon fibre
A strong but lightweight material made of tiny strands of carbon.

catapult
A device used to launch planes from aircraft carriers.

decommission
To end a ship's period of active service. The day of decommissioning is usually marked by a formal ceremony.

displacement
The amount of water that a ship moves out of the way when it floats on the sea.

escort
A ship that sails with other ships and protects them from attack.

fleet
A large group of warships, containing many different types of ship.

hull
The body of a ship.

Kevlar
A very strong artificial material that is used to make armour.

knot
The unit used to measure a ship's speed. One knot is one nautical mile per hour.

propeller
A kind of screw at the back of a ship that rotates to push the ship forwards. A ship may have several propellers that are powered by the ship's engines.

radar
A system that uses radio waves to detect other ships.

sonar
A system that uses sound waves to detect objects that are underwater.

stern
The rear part of a ship.

torpedo
A weapon with its own engine that is fired at targets underwater.

turbojet
An engine that uses gas turbines to produce power.

Ships at a glance

Ship	Years in Service	Number Built	Did You Know?
HMS *Warrior*	1861–1883	1	The ship was made as a show of strength to France. it never needed to fight a major battle.
Iowa class battleship	1943–1992	4	The battleships' nine main guns were housed in three turrets. It took more than 85 men to operate each turret.
Nimitz class aircraft carrier	1975–present	10	The aircraft carrier has four bronze propellers. Each propeller is 8 metres in diameter and weighs 30 tonnes.
Oliver Hazard Perry class frigate	1977–present	71	During bad weather, helicopters land on deck using a hook and cable system that pulls them safely down.
Skjold class patrol boat	1999–present	3	The catamaran design traps air between the two hulls. This 'air cushion' allows the ship to go fast.
Wasp class amphibious assault ship	1989–present	8	Inside the ship, crew members move vehicles from storage areas to the well deck on monorail trains.
Astute class submarine	2010–present	2	The submarines carry missiles that can be fired at targets more than 2,000 kilometres away.

Websites

www.hms-victory.com

The official website for HMS *Victory*, with information about the museum ship and activities for schools.

www.hmswarrior.org

The website for HMS *Warrior*, featuring a virtual tour, and stories of life on board the ship.

www.submarine-museum.co.uk

The Royal Navy Submarine Museum's website, with information about its collection and ideas for projects.

www.navy.mil/navydata/ships/carriers/carriers.asp

The US Navy's guide to aircraft carriers, telling the story of these giant ships from their early years to today, and with profiles of the different crew members and their duties.

www.world-war.co.uk/index.php3

A website dedicated to warships from World War II. It contains a large number of historical photos, plus a wealth of information about the ships used by the navies involved in the war.

Index